20 AMAZING WOMEN EVERY GIRL SHOULD KNOW

REBEL GIRLS

Good Night Stories for Rebel Girls and Rebel Girls are registered trademarks.
Good Night Stories for Rebel Girls and all other Rebel Girls titles are available for bulk purchase for sale promotions, premiums, fundraising, and educational needs.
For details, write to sales@rebelgirls.com.

This is a work of creative nonfiction. It is a collection of heartwarming and thought-provoking stories inspired by the life and adventures of 20 influential women. It is not an encyclopedic account of the events and accomplishments of their lives.

www.rebelgirls.com

Parts of this work have been previously published in the books *Good Night Stories for Rebel Girls*, *Good Night Stories for Rebel Girls 2*, *Good Night Stories for Rebel Girls: 100 Immigrant Women Who Changed the World*, and *Rebel Girls Lead: 25 Tales of Powerful Women*.

Created by Francesca Cavallo and Elena Favilli
Additional text by Abby Sher, Jestine Ware, and Andrea Debbink
Art direction by Giulia Flamini
Graphic design by Annalisa Ventura

First published 2021
Printed in China
10 9 8 7 6 5 4 3 2 1

MIX
From responsible sources
FSC® C124807

CONTENTS

ADA LOVELACE

MATHEMATICIAN

Once upon a time, there was a girl named Ada who loved machines. She also loved the idea of flying.

She studied birds to work out the perfect balance between wing size and body weight. She tested out materials and tried out several designs. She never managed to soar like a bird, but she created a beautiful book full of drawings called *Flyology* where she recorded all of her findings.

One night, Ada went to a ball. There, she met a grumpy old mathematician named Charles Babbage. Ada was a brilliant mathematician herself, and the two soon became good friends. Charles invited Ada to see a machine he had invented. He called it the Difference Engine. It could automatically add and subtract numbers. No one had ever done that before.

Ada was hooked.

"What if we built a machine that could make more complicated calculations?" she said. Excited, Ada and Charles started working. Their machine was huge. It required an enormous steam engine.

Ada wanted to go further: "What if this machine could play music and show letters as well as numbers?"

She was describing a computer, way before modern computers were invented!

Ada wrote the first computer program in history.

DECEMBER 10, 1815–NOVEMBER 27, 1852

UNITED KINGDOM

· 4 ·

"THAT BRAIN OF MINE IS
SOMETHING MORE THAN MERELY
MORTAL, AS TIME WILL SHOW."
—ADA LOVELACE

AMELIA EARHART

AVIATOR

Once upon a time, a girl named Amelia saved enough money to buy a yellow airplane. She called it the *Canary*.

A few years later, she became the first woman to fly solo across the Atlantic Ocean. It was a dangerous flight. Her tiny plane was tossed around by strong winds and icy storms. She kept herself going with a can of tomato juice, sucked through a straw. After almost 15 hours, she touched down in a field in Northern Ireland, much to the surprise of the cows. When a few farmers came out to see what was going on, Amelia blurted out: "I'm from America!"

Amelia loved to fly, and she loved to do things no one had ever done before. Her biggest wish was to be the first woman to fly around the world.

She took only a small bag, as all the space in the plane had to be used for fuel. Her long flight was going well. She was supposed to land on the tiny Howland Island but never got there.

In her last transmission, Amelia said she was flying through clouds and was running low on fuel. Her plane disappeared somewhere over the Pacific Ocean and was never found.

Before leaving, she wrote, "I am quite aware of the hazards. I want to do it because I want to do it. Women must try to do the same things that men have tried. If they fail, their failure must be a challenge to others."

JULY 24, 1897–CIRCA JULY 2, 1937

UNITED STATES OF AMERICA

ILLUSTRATION BY
GIULIA FLAMINI

"ADVENTURE IS
WORTHWHILE IN ITSELF."
—AMELIA EARHART

BEYONCÉ

SINGER, SONGWRITER, AND BUSINESSWOMAN

Beyoncé was six years old when her dad started selling people tickets to go to their house and see her sing and dance. When Beyoncé told her mom she wanted to create a band with her friends, her mom said, "Okay. I'll make your costumes." And so Destiny's Child was born.

Beyoncé was the queen of the band. She was driven, focused, and interested in learning every aspect of the music business.

At first, her dad was her manager. But when she decided she wanted to be in control of her career, Beyoncé asked him to step aside. She didn't *just* want to be a popular singer—she wanted to be a powerhouse. And that's what she became.

One album at a time, Beyoncé forged her own path. She sang about freedom, about love, about independence, and about pain—both personal pain and social injustice. She inspired millions of Black women to be proud of their culture, their origins, and their own unique style.

When Beyoncé was asked to perform during the halftime show of the Super Bowl, she entered the stadium leading an army of female dancers all dressed in black. With her song "Formation," she dropped a Black power anthem in front of 100 million viewers.

Today, she is the most influential living pop star in the world.

BORN SEPTEMBER 4, 1981

UNITED STATES OF AMERICA

"WE ALL HAVE MORE POWER
THAN WE REALIZE."
—BEYONCÉ

FRIDA KAHLO

PAINTER

Once upon a time, in a bright blue house near Mexico City, there lived a small girl called Frida. She would grow up to be one of the most famous painters of the 20th century, but she almost didn't grow up at all.

When she was six, she nearly died from polio. The disease left her with a permanent limp, but that didn't stop her from playing, swimming, and wrestling just like all the other kids.

Then, when she was 18, she was in a terrible bus accident. She almost died again—and again she spent months in bed. Her mother made her a special easel so she could paint while lying down. More than anything else, Frida loved to paint.

As soon as she was able to walk again, she went to see Mexico's most famous artist, Diego Rivera. "Are my paintings any good?" she asked. Her paintings were amazing: bold, bright, and beautiful. He fell in love with them—and he fell in love with Frida.

Diego and Frida got married. He was a big man in a large floppy hat. She looked tiny beside him. People called them "the elephant and the dove."

During her life, Frida painted hundreds of portraits of herself, often surrounded by the monkeys, dogs, and birds that were her pets. The bright blue house where she lived has been kept just as she left it, full of color and joy and flowers.

JULY 6, 1907–JULY 13, 1954

MEXICO

"FEET, WHAT DO I NEED
YOU FOR WHEN I HAVE
WINGS TO FLY?"
—FRIDA KAHLO

GRETA THUNBERG

CLIMATE ACTIVIST

Greta didn't think like most kids. She'd been diagnosed with Asperger's syndrome and obsessive compulsive disorder (OCD). These conditions sometimes made her feel lonely, but they also allowed her to see the world in her own way.

At school, Greta watched a documentary about pollution in the oceans. She learned that a massive pile of plastic the size of Mexico was floating in the Pacific Ocean. When the movie ended, other students went on with their day, but Greta saw what no one else could: an urgent crisis.

First, Greta reduced her own carbon footprint. She stopped riding in planes and cars, saved energy by turning off electrical outlets in her home, and stopped eating meat or dairy products.

But small changes weren't enough. After all, Greta was just one person. How could she stop heat waves, storms, and wildfires alone? Instead of giving up because the problem was too big, Greta marched to the Swedish parliament. She refused to go back to school unless her country reduced its carbon emissions.

After that, she protested every Friday and spread her message on social media. Inspired by Greta, thousands of students from more than 100 countries walked out of school too. They sent their message to world leaders: the world is in trouble, and officials need to do something about it before it's too late.

BORN JANUARY 3, 2003

SWEDEN

ILLUSTRATION BY
KATERINA VORONINA

"I DON'T WANT YOUR
HOPE. I DON'T WANT
YOU TO BE HOPEFUL. I
WANT YOU TO PANIC."
—GRETA THUNBERG

HARRIET TUBMAN

FREEDOM FIGHTER

One day, 12-year-old Araminta was standing in front of a grocery store when a Black man came running past. He was being chased by a white man who yelled, "Stop that man! He's my slave!" She did nothing. She, too, was enslaved, and she hoped the man would escape.

Just then, the overseer hurled a heavy object at the man. He missed but hit Araminta on the head. She was injured, but her thick hair cushioned the blow enough to save her life. "My hair had never been combed," she said, "and it stood out like a bushel basket."

A few years later, she married a man named John Tubman and changed her name to Harriet after her mother. Harriet found out that she was going to be put up for sale, so she decided to escape.

Harriet hid in the daytime and traveled by night. When she crossed the border into Pennsylvania, she realized for the first time in her life she was free. "I looked at my hands to see if I was the same person now that I was free. There was such a glory over everything . . . I felt like I was in heaven."

She thought about the man she saw escaping and her family in Maryland who were still enslaved. She knew she had to help them. Over the next 11 years, she went back 19 times and rescued hundreds of enslaved people.

She was never captured, and she never lost a single person.

CIRCA 1822–MARCH 10, 1913

UNITED STATES OF AMERICA

"I HAVE HEARD THEIR GROANS AND
SIGHS AND SEEN THEIR TEARS, AND I
WOULD GIVE EVERY DROP OF BLOOD
IN MY VEINS TO FREE THEM."
—HARRIET TUBMAN

JANE GOODALL

PRIMATOLOGIST

Jane loved climbing trees and reading books. Her dream was to go to Africa and spend time with the wild animals there. So she left England and traveled to Tanzania with her notebook and binoculars, determined to study real chimpanzees in their natural environment.

At first, it was hard to get close to them. The chimpanzees would run away the moment she was in sight. But Jane kept visiting the same place every day at the same time. Eventually, the chimps allowed her to get closer. But Jane wanted to become friends with them. So she started a "banana club." Whenever she visited the chimpanzees, she would share bananas with them.

At the time, little was known about chimpanzees. Some scientists observed them from far away, using binoculars. Others studied them in cages. Jane, however, spent hours hanging out with chimpanzees. She tried to speak to them using grunts and cries. She climbed trees and ate the same foods they ate. She discovered that chimpanzees have rituals, that they make and use tools, and that they communicate using at least 120 different sounds. She even discovered that chimpanzees are not vegetarians.

Once, Jane rescued an injured chimpanzee and nursed it back to health. When she released it back into the wild, it turned and gave her a long, loving hug as if to say, "thanks and bye!"

BORN APRIL 3, 1934

UNITED KINGDOM

ILLUSTRATION BY
EMMANUELLE WALKER

"ONLY IF WE UNDERSTAND, WILL
WE CARE. ONLY IF WE CARE,
WILL WE HELP. ONLY IF WE
HELP, SHALL ALL BE SAVED."
—JANE GOODALL

KAMALA HARRIS

VICE PRESIDENT

Once there was a girl who attended civil rights marches before she was even born. Later, her parents, who were originally from India and Jamaica, took her to protests where they shouted chants while wide-eyed Kamala watched from her stroller.

Eventually, Kamala outgrew the stroller and ventured onto the streets of Oakland, California, on her own. She knew she wanted to be someone who could help others in times of trouble.

Kamala went to Howard University, in Washington, DC, and followed in the footsteps of many famous Black lawyers. She took an internship on Capitol Hill. Every day, she walked by the Supreme Court building. On it, the words "Equal Justice Under Law" were etched into the stone. Kamala thought about how to make sure those words were true for everyone.

As a lawyer, she battled fierce adversaries with her words. Then she became the first-ever female district attorney in the San Francisco Bay Area, beating out her old boss for the job. She later ran for attorney general of the whole state of California—and won!

Then Kamala climbed even higher. She was elected to the US Senate. And, in 2020, former vice president Joe Biden chose her as his running mate when he ran for president. The powerful pair won the election, and Kamala became the first woman, the first Black person, and the first South Asian person to ever hold that office.

BORN OCTOBER 20, 1968

UNITED STATES OF AMERICA

ILLUSTRATION BY
NICOLE MILES

"WHILE I MAY BE THE
FIRST WOMAN IN THIS
OFFICE, I WON'T BE
THE LAST."
—KAMALA HARRIS

LADY GAGA

SINGER AND ACTIVIST

Once there was a girl named Stefani who used music to survive. At school, she was bullied. At home, she fought with her dad. But at the piano, she felt like she could change the world.

She started playing piano when she was four years old and was performing in a nightclub by the time she was 14. Stefani created her own songs and dreamed up her own style. She was loud, bright, and fierce. Onstage, she wore bedazzled bikinis, face paint, and wigs. And she called herself Lady Gaga.

In 2008, Lady Gaga released her first single. People loved it! Her next hit song topped the charts in almost every country. As she got more and more popular, her outfits and performances got wilder. One time, she dove from the roof of a football stadium. Another time, she wore a dress made of raw meat!

But as she got older, Lady Gaga realized, "The most shocking thing I can possibly do is be completely vulnerable and honest." She started talking to the press about how she was abused as a teenager and was in treatment to deal with her trauma.

Lady Gaga wanted to help other people who were hurting too. She started the Born This Way Foundation, which helps young people talk about mental illness. From then on, she encouraged everyone to spread acts of kindness.

BORN MARCH 28, 1986

UNITED STATES OF AMERICA

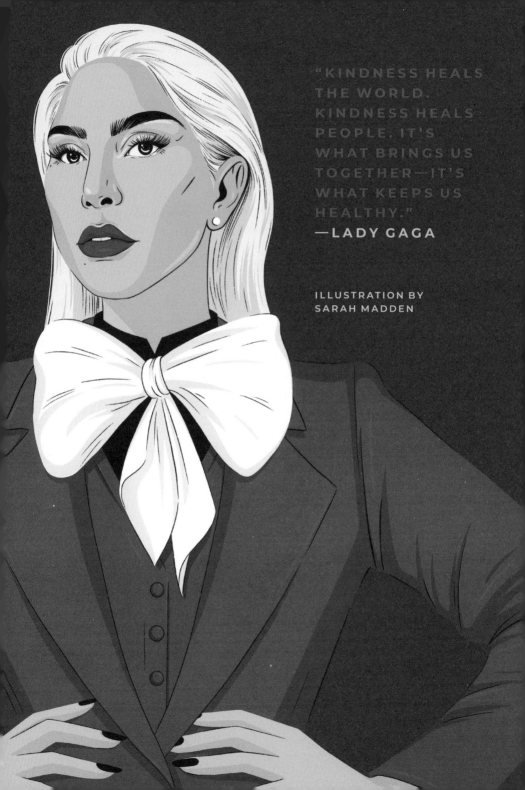

"KINDNESS HEALS THE WORLD. KINDNESS HEALS PEOPLE. IT'S WHAT BRINGS US TOGETHER—IT'S WHAT KEEPS US HEALTHY."
—LADY GAGA

ILLUSTRATION BY SARAH MADDEN

MAE C. JEMISON

ASTRONAUT AND DOCTOR

Once there was a curious girl named Mae who couldn't make up her mind about what she wanted to be.

Sewing dresses for her Barbie dolls, she wanted to be a fashion designer. Reading a book about space travel, she wanted to be an astronaut. Fixing a broken toy, she thought maybe an engineer would be better. And going to the theater, she exclaimed, "Maybe I'll become a dancer."

The world was Mae's laboratory. She studied engineering, African American studies, and medicine. She learned to speak Russian, Swahili, and Japanese. She became a doctor and volunteered in Cambodia and Sierra Leone. Then she applied to NASA to become an astronaut. Mae was selected, and after one year of training, she was sent into space on board the space shuttle *Endeavour*.

Since she was both an astronaut and a doctor, her mission was to conduct experiments on things like weightlessness and motion sickness, which can be a problem when you're floating upside down in space!

When Mae came back to Earth, she realized that—while she had enjoyed space—her true passion was improving health in Africa. So she quit NASA and founded a company that uses satellites to do just that.

Mae Jemison was the first Black woman in space.

BORN OCTOBER 17, 1956

UNITED STATES OF AMERICA

ILLUSTRATION BY
ALEXANDRA BOWMAN

"ONE THING I WAS
CONSISTENT ABOUT WAS
TESTING LIMITS—MINE
AND OTHER PEOPLE'S—
ESPECIALLY ADULTS."
—MAE C. JEMISON

MALALA YOUSAFZAI

EDUCATION ACTIVIST

Once there was a girl named Malala who loved school. Malala lived in a peaceful valley in Pakistan. One day, a group of armed men called the Taliban took control of the valley. They frightened people with their guns. They also forbade girls from going to school. Many people disagreed, but they thought it would be safer to keep their girls at home.

Malala thought this was unfair, and wrote about it online. She loved school very much—so one day, she said on TV, "Education is power for women. The Taliban are closing girls' schools because they don't want women to be powerful."

A short while later, Malala got onto her school bus as usual. Suddenly, two Taliban men stopped the bus and shouted, "Which one of you is Malala?"

When her friends looked at her, the men fired their guns, hitting her in the head and injuring two other girls too. Malala was rushed to the hospital. Thousands of children sent her get well cards. She recovered faster than anyone could've imagined.

"They thought bullets would silence us, but they failed," she said. "Let us pick up our books and our pens. They are our most powerful weapons. One child, one teacher, one book, and one pen can change the world."

Malala is the youngest person to receive the Nobel Peace Prize.

BORN JULY 12, 1997

PAKISTAN

MAYA ANGELOU

WRITER

Once there was a little girl who didn't speak for five years. She thought her words could hurt people and promised to never make a peep again. Her name was Maya.

People thought Maya was crazy, but she was simply scared. "I know you will speak again one day," her grandmother kept telling her. "You will find your voice," her beloved brother said.

Maya listened to them and began to memorize everything she heard or read: poems, songs, short tales, random conversations. "It was like putting a CD on. If I wanted to, I'd run through my memory and think, that's the one I want to hear," she later recalled.

She became so good at memorizing words that when she started to write, it was like music was flowing from her pen. She wrote about her childhood, growing up in a town where Black people were treated badly for the color of their skin.

Her writing became the voice of the civil rights movement and all the people fighting for the rights of Black Americans. She constantly reminded us that everyone, Black or white, male or female, has equal rights.

In addition to writing books, Maya wrote songs, plays, and movies, and acted onstage and onscreen. "See me now, Black, female, American, and Southern," she once said to a group of Black students. "See me and see yourselves. What can't you do?"

APRIL 4, 1928–MAY 28, 2014

UNITED STATES OF AMERICA

"MY MISSION IN LIFE IS NOT MERELY TO SURVIVE, BUT TO THRIVE, AND TO DO SO WITH SOME PASSION, SOME COMPASSION, SOME HUMOR, AND SOME STYLE."
—MAYA ANGELOU

MICHELLE KWAN

FIGURE SKATER

Once there was a girl who floated through fields of gold. Her name was Michelle. From the time she was five years old, she knew she wanted to be an ice skater. Sometimes she went to sleep in her skates so she could get on the ice before dawn. Every day, she practiced her leaps and lutzes, trying out new moves. And at age six, she won her first competition.

Michelle's parents were thrilled but also concerned. They were both juggling multiple jobs while running a family restaurant. There was no money for sparkly costumes or brand-new skates. Michelle told them none of that mattered. Who needs fancy skates and sequins to land a double axel?

Her dedication paid off. In 1998, Michelle went to the Olympics, where she won a silver medal. Four years later, she went to the Olympics for a second time. Her graceful performance mesmerized the audience. Even after she fell during one of her routines, she picked herself up and skated on, earning a bronze medal.

Michelle won more than 40 championships, including five world titles. But as Michelle says, "Medals don't really mean that much. It's the experience, the story of the skating, the love."

And as she sailed across the ice for her last Olympic program, set to the song "Fields of Gold," everyone could feel the love coursing through her arms and legs and shining in her radiant smile.

BORN JULY 7, 1980

UNITED STATES OF AMERICA

ILLUSTRATION BY
LILY KIM QIAN

"I DIDN'T LOSE THE GOLD.
I WON THE SILVER."
—MICHELLE KWAN

MICHELLE OBAMA

LAWYER AND FIRST LADY

O nce upon a time, there was a girl who was always afraid. Her name was Michelle Robinson, and she lived in a tiny apartment in Chicago with her family.

"Maybe I'm not smart enough," she worried. "Maybe I'm not good enough." And her mother would say, "If it can be done, you can do it."

"Anything is possible," said her dad.

Michelle worked hard. But still, sometimes people told her not to aim too high. They said she would never achieve something big because "she was just a Black girl from the South Side of Chicago."

But Michelle chose to listen to her parents. "Anything is possible," she thought. So she graduated from Harvard and became a lawyer at a big firm. One day, her boss asked her to mentor a young lawyer. His name was Barack Hussein Obama.

They fell in love and got married a few years later.

Eventually, Barack told her he wanted to become President of the United States. At first, she thought he was crazy, but then she remembered: "If it can be done, you can do it." So she quit her job and helped him on his campaign.

Barack won the election, and Michelle became the first Black First Lady of the United States. "No one is born smart," she likes to point out. "All of that comes with a lot of hard work."

BORN JANUARY 17, 1964

UNITED STATES OF AMERICA

"ALWAYS STAY TRUE TO
YOURSELF AND NEVER LET
WHAT SOMEBODY ELSE SAYS
DISTRACT YOU FROM
YOUR GOALS."
—MICHELLE OBAMA

ILLUSTRATION BY
MARTA SIGNORI

OPRAH WINFREY

TV HOST AND BUSINESSWOMAN

Once there was a girl named Oprah who loved to talk. But her family didn't listen. Her mother brushed her away, saying, "Be quiet! I don't have time for you." Her grandmother never let her cry. "People will think you're weak," she said.

But keeping everything bottled up inside was unbearable.

So Oprah kept looking for opportunities to speak out. First, she joined the public speaking team in high school. Then she worked at a local radio station. Eventually, she joined a Baltimore TV news show as a co-anchor.

Her family and friends were excited. But deep inside, Oprah wasn't sure that reporting the news was what she loved the most.

After being fired from the show, she was given a low-rated early morning talk show. Oprah thought her career was over. Instead, while interviewing an ice cream seller, she discovered her greatest talent: connecting with compassion. People started to love the show because she really listened to her guests. If they cried, she felt their sadness. If they were angry, she understood their pain. And if they were happy, she laughed with them.

Oprah became the queen of talk shows. She moved on to national television. She launched her own TV network and became a multi-billionaire and one of the most generous philanthropists in history.

BORN JANUARY 29, 1954

UNITED STATES OF AMERICA

"YOU GET IN LIFE WHAT YOU HAVE
THE COURAGE TO ASK FOR."
—OPRAH WINFREY

ILLUSTRATION BY
T.S. ABE

RIHANNA

ENTREPRENEUR AND SINGER

O nce there was a girl who wanted her music to be heard all over the world. When Rihanna was a teenager, she auditioned for a record label. The producers were so impressed they encouraged her to move to the United States. Even though Rihanna loved Barbados and her family, she made the move.

After she arrived in the US, the record label offered her a contract, and her career took off. Her songs played on the radio and fans lined up to see her onstage. Yet it took a while for Rihanna to find her true voice. In Barbadian culture, Rihanna said, being quiet was considered polite. But in the US, her quietness was seen as rude. "You mean well, and it can come across in a different way in a different culture."

Rihanna won nine Grammy Awards and became one of the best-selling music artists of all time. Her musical success opened doors into business. In 2017, Rihanna launched Fenty Beauty, a cosmetics brand that focused on inclusivity. She and her team spent two years developing foundation that came in a wide variety of skin tones—more than 40 shades. Her company's emphasis on diversity has inspired other cosmetics brands to do the same. Then in 2019, Rihanna created her own luxury fashion line.

"The thing that keeps me alive and passionate is being creative," Rihanna said.

BORN FEBRUARY 20, 1988

UNITED STATES OF AMERICA

"MUSIC HAD LED ME TO THESE OTHER OUTLETS, AND TO THINGS I GENUINELY LOVE."
—RIHANNA

ILLUSTRATION BY JESTENIA SOUTHERLAND

RUTH BADER GINSBURG

SUPREME COURT JUSTICE

Once upon a time, there was a girl who dreamed of becoming a great lawyer. "A lady lawyer?" people said. "Don't be ridiculous! Lawyers and judges are always men."

Ruth looked around her and saw that they were right. But she attended Harvard Law School and Columbia Law School just the same. Her husband, Marty, was also a student at Harvard. "Your wife should be home baking cookies and looking after the baby," people would say. Marty didn't listen. Ruth was a terrible cook! Besides, he loved taking care of their daughter, and he was proud of his brilliant wife.

Ruth was passionate about women's rights. She argued six landmark cases on gender equality before the United States Supreme Court. Then she became the second female Supreme Court justice in the country's history.

There are nine justices on the Supreme Court. "If I'm asked when will there be enough women on the Supreme Court, I say, 'When there are nine,'" explained Ruth. "People are shocked—but there've been nine men, like forever, and nobody's ever raised their eyebrows at that."

Even in her eighties, Ruth did 20 push-ups every day and became a style icon, thanks to the extravagant collars she wore in court with her judge's robes.

MARCH 15, 1933–SEPTEMBER 18, 2020

UNITED STATES OF AMERICA

ILLUSTRATION BY
ELEANOR DAVIS

"I DISSENT."
—RUTH BADER GINSBURG

SERENA WILLIAMS

TENNIS PLAYER

Once there was a girl named Serena who loved dressing up in tutus and speaking her mind. She was the youngest of five daughters who all shared a single bedroom in Compton, California. When she was three, her dad opened up a new world for her and her sister Venus. He taught them to play tennis.

He also asked some of the local kids to come by the public courts and boo at the girls while they practiced. That way, they'd learn how to focus and believe in themselves. It was the most important lesson of Serena's life.

Serena started playing professionally when she was just 14 years old. Soon she was collecting titles and trophies all over the world. Sometimes she played doubles with Venus, and sometimes the sisters were paired off against each other. No matter what, they always cheered each other on. By 2002, Serena was ranked first in the world. And by 2017, she'd won 23 Grand Slam single titles!

Serena became a leader off the court too. She speaks out for human rights and demands that all athletes are treated equally, regardless of gender or skin color. She's also created the Serena Williams Foundation to build schools in Jamaica and Africa.

And as for those tutus she loves? Her Serena fashion line has clothes for all body types. Serena is a mom too. She and her daughter can be seen in matching frills practicing their serves.

 BORN SEPTEMBER 26, 1981

UNITED STATES OF AMERICA

"I'VE GROWN MOST NOT FROM VICTORIES, BUT SETBACKS."
—SERENA WILLIAMS

ILLUSTRATION BY CAMILLA RU

SIMONE BILES

GYMNAST

Once there was a girl who loved pasta, shopping, and bounding across gymnastics mats doing back handsprings and flips. Her name was Simone.

Simone was born in Ohio but went to live with her grandparents in Texas when she was very young. One day, on a school field trip, Simone visited a gymnastics center and started imitating the moves she saw. The coach sent home a letter saying she should start training with them, and when she was six years old, she did.

She leaped and spun, catapulting across the mats, balance beams, and vaults and whirling around the uneven bars. She started competing and won medal after medal.

By the time she was 16, Simone became the first Black woman to win gold in the all-around competition at the World Championships. Her smile gleamed even brighter than her bedazzled leotard as she accepted the award.

Today, Simone is the most decorated gymnast in US history, with 30 major medals—many of them gold! But she never lets these medals weigh her down. She is always coming up with new ways to flip and fly, twist and soar. A strong, daring, and creative gymnast, Simone invents new routines and moves that no one has ever tried before. On the floor, the "Biles II" is a triple twisting double backflip, and it always ends with a great big grin.

BORN MARCH 14, 1997

UNITED STATES OF AMERICA

ILLUSTRATION BY
ELINE VAN DAM

"I'D RATHER REGRET THE
RISKS THAT DIDN'T WORK
OUT THAN THE CHANCES
I DIDN'T TAKE AT ALL."
—SIMONE BILES

STACEY ABRAMS

ACTIVIST AND POLITICIAN

O nce there was a girl named Stacey who loved hip-hop, *Star Trek*, and climbing trees. She was one of six children, and her parents couldn't always afford electricity. Still, her family showed up for school, church, and volunteering at soup kitchens. They believed there was always a way to help others.

Stacey got the highest grades. She was named valedictorian of her high school. Part of her prize was a visit with the governor. He lived in a mansion with huge gates and a guard who said Stacey didn't belong there. She didn't know if he said that because she had brown skin or because she looked poor. She didn't care what his reason was. She just knew, from that moment on, that she wanted "to be the person who got to open the gates."

Stacey earned a law degree, wrote novels, started two small businesses, and became a lawmaker in Georgia. In 2018, Stacey ran for governor of Georgia. She was the first Black woman to do this for a major political party. She got more votes than any other Democrat in the state's history. But her opponent made sure that a lot of people weren't allowed to vote, and Stacey lost.

Stacey didn't quit. She channeled her frustration into inspiration. For two years, she dedicated herself to making voting easier. She also registered 800,000 voters in Georgia—because she believes that everyone's voice matters, and she will open those gates for all.

BORN DECEMBER 9, 1973

UNITED STATES OF AMERICA

ILLUSTRATION BY
KELSEE THOMAS

"LEADERSHIP IS
ABOUT ANSWERING
THAT QUESTION: HOW
CAN I HELP?"
—STACEY ABRAMS

WRITE YOUR STORY

Once upon a time, _____

_____

_____

_____

_____

_____

_____

_____

_____

_____

_____

_____

_____

_____

_____

_____

_____

_____

_____

_____

_____

_____

_____

_____

DRAW YOUR PORTRAIT

ABOUT REBEL GIRLS

REBEL GIRLS is a global, multi-platform entertainment brand dedicated to inspiring and instilling confidence in a generation of girls around the world. Rebel Girls started from a 2016 international best-selling children's book featuring real-life, extraordinary women throughout history, geography, and fields of excellence, focusing on creators, innovators, leaders, and champions. In addition to its best-selling book series, Rebel Girls creates an award-winning, chart-topping podcast, brought to life by the voices of phenomenal current-day women. Rebel Girls also offers virtual experiences and toys and is expanding its reach to television, live theater, and a digital app. Its community of self-identified Rebel Girls spans more than 100 countries, with 6 million books sold in 51 languages and 15 million podcast downloads.

Join the Rebel Girls' community:
 Facebook: facebook.com/rebelgirls
 Instagram: @rebelgirls
 Twitter: @rebelgirlsbook
 Web: rebelgirls.com
 Podcast: rebelgirls.com/podcast

ILLUSTRATORS

Nineteen extraordinary female artists from all over the world illustrated the portraits in this book. Here are their names.

ALEXANDRA BOWMAN, **USA**, 23

CAMILLA RU, **UK**, 39

ELEANOR DAVIS, **USA**, 37

ELINE VAN DAM, **NETHERLANDS**, 9, 41

ELISABETTA STOINICH, **ITALY**, 5

EMMANUELLE WALKER, **CANADA**, 17

GIULIA FLAMINI, **ITALY**, 7

HELENA MORAIS SOARES, **PORTUGAL**, 11

JESTENIA SOUTHERLAND, **USA**, 35

KATERINA VORONINA, **GERMANY**, 13

KELSEE THOMAS, **USA**, 43

LILY KIM QIAN, **CANADA**, 29

MARTA SIGNORI, **ITALY**, 31

NICOLE MILES, **THE BAHAMAS**, 19

SALLY NIXON, **USA**, 15

SARA BONDI, **ITALY**, 25

SARAH MADDEN, **UK**, 21

T.S. ABE, **UK**, 33

THANDIWE TSHABALALA, **SOUTH AFRICA**, 27

CELEBRATE MORE AMAZING WOMEN!

ACTIVITY BOOK

Good Night Stories for Rebel Girls and Rebel Girls are registered trademarks. *Good Night Stories for Rebel Girls* and all other Rebel Girls titles are available for bulk purchase for sale promotions, premiums, fundraising, and educational needs. For details, write to sales@rebelgirls.com.

www.rebelgirls.com

Created by Francesca Cavallo and Elena Favilli
Art direction by Giulia Flamini
Cover illustrations and graphic design by Annalisa Ventura
Activities by Sarah Parvis
Coloring pages by Elisabetta Stoinich
Other illustration credits: 4: Helena Morais Soares, 6–7: Barbara Dziadosz, 8: Giulia Flamini, 10: Elisa Seitzinger, 15: Keturah Ariel, 16: Trudi-Ann Hemans, 20: Nicole Miles, 22: Annalisa Ventura, 26–27: Martina Paukova, 30: Lisk Feng, 34–35: Alexandra Bowman, 39: Decue Wu, 40: Kate Prior, 42–43: Marijke Buurlage, 45: Amanda Hall

Printed in China
First printing 2021
10 9 8 7 6 5 4 3 2 1

Frida Kahlo

WHAT MAKES A REBEL A REBEL?

Rebel Girls exist all over the world! Some get started very young, like skateboarder Sky Brown. Others like poet Cora Coralina, accomplish great things later in life. But these inspiring women share many qualities. They are brave and bold. They stand up to injustice and raise their voices to make the world a better place. With kindness and compassion, they care for their communities and help keep children safe. They study and train hard to do incredible things on the court, in the lab, on the stage, or in the halls of government. They use their intelligence and ingenuity to uncover new things about the world.

Many Rebel Girls have experienced challenges in their lives. Some have been discriminated against because of their gender or the color of their skin. Some have been born into poverty, lived through war, or overcome illness or injury. Filled with determination and resilience, these women have made their mark on the world.

Let's honor the creativity, curiosity, strength, and leadership of amazing women, from scientist Marie Curie and painter Frida Kahlo to soccer star Megan Rapinoe and Vice President Kamala Harris. And let's celebrate the next generation of Rebels who are just getting started! You are never too young to shoot for the stars!

· 4 ·

A	V	F	I	W	G	X	D	J	I	A	Q	W	O	L
C	O	M	M	U	N	I	T	I	E	S	C	A	L	H
H	I	C	G	U	B	L	C	S	R	A	T	S	E	I
A	C	S	A	E	N	U	R	K	E	P	J	F	A	N
L	E	R	X	D	P	V	E	V	B	Q	S	L	D	G
L	S	K	E	J	A	H	A	Z	E	S	T	L	E	E
E	B	I	R	L	O	R	T	F	L	T	R	A	R	N
N	E	N	O	U	B	G	I	K	C	O	E	C	S	U
G	J	D	C	Q	M	O	V	U	W	Y	N	E	H	I
E	I	N	S	P	I	R	I	N	G	R	G	A	I	T
S	H	E	R	A	B	K	T	S	W	Z	T	E	P	Y
F	O	S	B	O	L	D	Y	X	D	R	H	Q	A	O
U	E	S	V	E	J	B	N	W	E	D	V	H	O	M
L	H	I	K	E	C	N	E	I	L	I	S	E	R	G
P	O	Z	A	L	T	S	A	X	C	W	K	U	D	B

· 5 ·

WHAT'S COOKING?

Julia Child was a spy before she became a famous chef! She was constantly learning and changing. This picture has been changing too! Can you spot 7 things that are different?

SPOT THE IMPOSTER!

Amelia Earhart set records as an aviator. She was the first woman to fly across the Atlantic Ocean by herself. Sadly, she went missing while attempting to be the first woman to fly around the entire globe. Something is missing in the pictures below too. Which picture is not like the others?

Elizabeth Tudor

READY TO RHYME?

Emily Dickinson, Claudia Rankine, and Wisława Szymborska are talented poets whose words have moved countless people. Are you a poet too? Not all poems rhyme, but it's still fun to test your rhyming skills! What rhymes with CORE?

Diane von Fürstenberg is a fashion designer. She became famous for the clothes she designed and W O R E.

Many young Rebels earn an allowance. They earn money for every _____ they do.

Marta Vieira da Silva is an incredible soccer player. When she shoots for the goal, she shoots to _ _ _ _ _.

Kristal Ambrose is an environmentalist who wants to keep her beaches clean. She works hard to make sure no plastic waste ends up in the water or on the _____.

Thandiwe Mweetwa protects and studies lions and other wildlife in Zambia. She knows that when lions want to be heard, they _ _ _ _.

Wangari Maathai started the Green Belt Movement, which has planted 51 million trees in Africa. That's an amazing number of trees, but she wants to plant even   .

Mary Anning was a fossil collector who uncovered the bones of dinosaurs. She knew a lot about the animals around her, but she was interested in the animals that came _ _ _ _ _ _.

Madam C.J. Walker created hair care products for Black women. She also hired and trained thousands of women to go out into neighborhoods and sell her products   to   .

Harriet Tubman helped hundreds of people escape from slavery. She also worked as a nurse and a spy during the Civil _ _ _ _.

CLIMB A WORD LADDER!

Use the missing word in each clue to build the ladder. Each word in the ladder is just one letter different from the words above and below.

When writer Toni Morrison was young, she discovered she loved to _ _ _ _.

r e a d

Ruth E. Carter is an award-winning costume designer. To decorate a dress, she might add a sequin, a bow, or a shiny, little _ _ _ _.

Florence Griffith Joyner was the fastest woman in the world. When she ran in a race, she could not be _ _ _ _.

Jessica Watson sailed around the world in a bright pink _ _ _ _.

Mary Edwards Walker was a surgeon during the US Civil War. She did not wear corsets and petticoats like most women. She wore shirts, pants, and ties. On her foot, instead of a high-heeled shoe, she wore a _ _ _ _.

Beatrix Potter is a famous author who wrote for children. *The Tale of Peter Rabbit* was her very first _ _ _ _.

CRACK THE CODE

Use the key below to help reveal inspiring quotations from Rebel women.

A	**B**	**C**	**D**
E	**F**	**G**	
H	**I**	**J**	**K**
L	**M**	**N**	
O	**P**	**Q**	**R**
S	**T**	**U**	
V	**W**	**X**	**Y**
Z			

"As you ▢▢▢▢▢ ▢▢▢▢▢, you ▢▢▢▢ ▢▢▢▢▢▢▢▢ that you have ▢▢▢ ▢▢▢▢▢: one for ▢▢▢▢▢▢▢ ▢▢▢▢▢▢▢, the other for ▢▢▢▢▢▢▢ ▢▢▢▢▢▢."

—Audrey Hepburn, actress

"I'd rather ▢▢▢▢ ▢▢▢▢▢▢ to ▢▢ ▢▢▢▢▢▢▢ in the ▢▢▢▢▢ than ▢▢▢▢▢ at ▢▢▢▢▢ ▢▢▢▢▢▢▢."

—Nadine Burke Harris, pediatrician

"Be ▢▢▢▢▢▢▢, be ▢▢▢▢▢▢, be ▢▢▢▢▢▢▢▢▢▢."

—Keiko Fukuda, judo master

"The ▢▢▢▢▢▢▢▢ that can ▢▢▢▢▢ ▢▢▢▢▢▢ is ▢▢▢▢▢▢▢."

—Amanda Gorman, poet

MODEL MIX-UP

Unlike most models, Clara Holmes shows off her style from a wheelchair. She's always experimenting with fashion. Which one of these looks is unlike the rest?

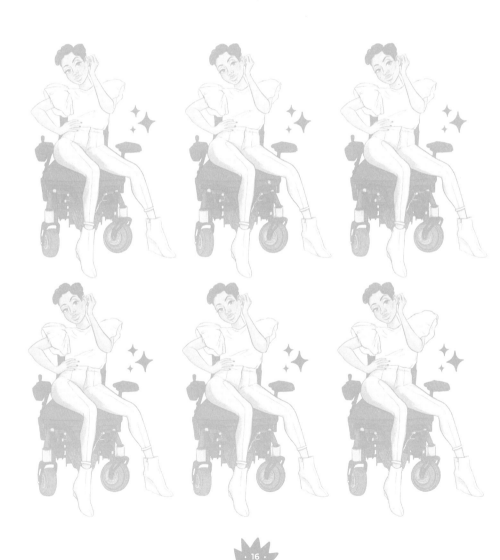

Marie Curie

MEET CARMEN MIRANDA

Carmen Miranda's real name is Maria. Her father gave her the nickname Carmen after a famous opera character. Born in Portugal, Carmen moved to Brazil as a baby. She started her career singing popular Brazilian songs. After her first record in 1930, she became a star! She sang and danced in movie musicals and was known for her unique look: colorful flowing dresses, platform shoes, and elaborate headdresses. She became the highest-paid actress in Hollywood.

All of the bold words above can be found in the puzzle below. They can go up, down, forward, backward, and even diagonally.

E	N	O	B	O	G	E	H	Z	A	C	Q	W	Y	H
J	E	G	M	U	S	I	C	A	L	S	P	A	A	P
A	M	I	C	H	I	A	J	K	E	I	O	S	O	S
D	R	A	D	E	M	O	U	S	T	A	R	F	L	B
O	A	C	T	R	E	S	S	O	C	N	T	L	S	I
O	C	I	L	O	R	E	I	D	S	A	U	L	U	F
W	E	F	B	H	R	C	N	V	B	E	G	A	M	S
Y	C	A	U	D	I	L	G	O	R	U	A	L	U	K
L	E	I	D	W	T	A	I	R	A	M	L	E	C	A
L	D	A	N	C	E	D	N	U	Z	C	A	A	S	I
O	E	U	I	E	Q	O	G	X	I	P	O	E	E	Z
H	E	M	A	N	K	C	I	N	L	A	F	Q	O	W

SPORTS SCRAMBLE!

Lisa Leslie is an amazing basketball player. Simone Biles is a champion gymnast. And Lorena Ochoa has been winning golf tournaments since she was seven. There are so many exciting sports to try out. Can you unscramble the sports words below? If you need help, you can find the words in the Hint Box.

LWBINGO

MWSI

GISNIK

RAWOBODSN

CORK BEMICRL

GUEFRI KTASE

ABBELLSA

KATBEBSLAL

OLFG

HINT BOX

SWIM
SKIING
SNOWBOARD
ROCK CLIMBER
GOLF
FIGURE SKATE
BOWLING
BASEBALL
BASKETBALL

· 19 ·

PATH TO THE WHITE HOUSE

Which way should she go? Help Kamala Harris navigate this maze and get her to her office in the White House.

Jane Austen

WISE WORDS

Use the key below to uncover uplifting thoughts from Rebel women.

A	B	C	D	E	F	G
H	I	J	K	L	M	N
O	P	Q	R	S	T	U
	V	W	X	Y	Z	

" Winning the prize wasn't half as exciting as doing the work itself."

—Maria Goeppert Mayer, theoretical physicist

—Beatrix Potter, author and illustrator

—Velma Scantlebury, transplant surgeon

GRACE HOPPER, COMPUTER PIONEER

Grace was a professor of math and physics. During World War II, she joined the Navy, where she was introduced to the first computer! Called "Mark I," it filled the entire room. But no one really knew how to use it. Grace studied it closely. It took a lot of hard work, but thanks to the programs Grace wrote, US forces were able to decode secret messages sent by their enemies during the war. Grace saved lives and became a respected computer expert.

All of the bold words above can be found in the puzzle below. They can go up, down, forward, backward, and even diagonally.

A	S	E	G	A	S	S	E	M	O	K	A	T	R	K
M	R	I	T	P	U	D	I	T	A	M	F	E	A	A
T	A	P	R	O	F	E	S	S	O	R	S	N	S	P
O	G	O	E	L	R	C	A	C	X	E	K	W	F	H
S	E	Q	P	I	Z	O	S	I	Q	U	R	I	L	E
U	B	U	X	S	C	D	Y	S	V	F	B	N	L	N
V	G	D	E	A	G	E	P	Y	I	C	A	D	A	I
W	I	R	W	O	K	H	C	H	V	E	G	O	L	Z
E	S	M	A	R	G	O	R	P	M	A	T	H	E	B
V	T	S	U	C	M	E	A	X	E	U	N	J	A	O
L	R	E	K	V	E	Z	W	U	P	Q	Y	I	E	R
O	A	N	O	S	T	U	D	I	E	D	C	X	Q	A

Mary Shelley

DIG IT!

Mary Anning had a knack for finding dinosaur fossils. In fact, she uncovered the first ichthyosaur skeleton. It was 30 feet long! Are you good at finding things too? Can you spot 8 things that have changed in this pair of pictures?

ADVENTURE JUMBLE

Explorer Mary Kingsley was the first woman to climb Mount Cameroon. Scientist Emilie Snethlage trekked deep into the Amazon rain forest. And retired nurse Barbara Hillary journeyed to the North and South Poles. There are so many wonderful places to explore! Somehow these words about exploration have gotten all mixed up. Can you unscramble the words below? If you need help, you can find the words in the Hint Box.

TOUNSMAIN

ESAS

UGSELJN

COSLENOVA

TNOHR LEOP

FWILIDEL

CONASE

SPAM

TEEDSSR

TIME TO RHYME!

TIME rhymes with RHYME. So does LIME, SLIME, and CLIMB. Show off your rhyming talent by filling in the blanks below with words that rhyme with POKE.

Sarinya Srisakul was the first female Asian American firefighter in New York City. She knows how to battle fire and _ _ _ _ _.

Daniela Soto-Innes is a celebrated Mexican chef. She spent many years as a pastry chef. When making desserts, she knows bakers often need to break open each egg and separate it into the egg white and the _ _ _ _ _.

Margaret Clay Ferguson was the first woman to be elected president of the Botanical Society of America. She knows a lot about trees, whether it is a maple, an elm, or a big strong _ _ _.

In the Harry Potter series, J.K. Rowling writes about a magical garment. Sometimes Harry and his friends wear an invisibility _ _ _ _ _ _ when they don't want to be seen.

Sometimes Olympic swimmer Regan Smith competes in freestyle or butterfly. But her best event is the b a c k _ _ _ _ _ _ . She holds the world record for the 100-meter and 200-meter races.

As a child, writer Maya Angelou did not talk for five years. She listened quietly and read countless books. When she finally _ _ _ _ _ _ again, she had an incredible memory and a love of storytelling.

Sprinter Wilma Rudolph made history when she _ _ _ _ _ _ three world records at the 1960 Olympics.

While sailing around the world, Jessica Watson often _ _ _ _ _ up to glorious sunrises before starting her day.

BUILD A WORD LADDER!

Use the clues below to figure out each missing word. Then add each missing word to the ladder. Each word in the ladder is just one letter different from the words above and below.

Grace O'Malley was a pirate. She captained a giant ship and loved to _ _ _ _.

Joan Wiffen found the first dinosaur fossil in New Zealand when she uncovered a long bone that was part of a theropod's _ _ _ _.

Marta Empinotti is a base jumper. She wears a parachute and leaps from places high above the ground, like bridges, cliffs, or _ _ _ _ buildings.

Isabel Allende is an author known for writing in a style called magical realism. She mixes fantasy into the realistic stories she likes to _ _ _ _.

Julia López is an Afro-Mexican painter known for her scenes of life in the countryside. Her paintings are bright with grassy greens, bright reddish-oranges, and blue-green colors like _ _ _ _.

t e a l

Alexa Canady is a neurosurgeon. She uses her knowledge and skills to diagnose brain disorders in children and help them _ _ _ _.

Ada Lovelace

ASTRONAUT ADJUSTMENTS

Mae Jemison was the first Black woman to fly into space. She knows the universe is always growing and changing. Guess what else is changing? This picture! Find 9 differences in this out-of-this-world puzzle.

ARETHA FRANKLIN, QUEEN OF SOUL

Aretha Franklin got her start singing in church as a child. She grew up and mastered all kinds of music. With her powerful voice and incredible talent, she sang breathtaking gospel, jazz, blues, pop, and R&B music. Once she even filled in for a famous opera singer when he was too sick to perform. She won 18 Grammy awards and was the first woman inducted into the Rock & Roll Hall of Fame.

All of the bold words above can be found in the puzzle below. They can go up, down, forward, backward, and even diagonally.

M	A	P	I	N	R	T	A	I	Z	O	B	K	A	W
I	Y	R	U	P	O	P	F	Z	H	D	A	G	H	A
V	S	P	C	A	C	U	A	M	U	S	I	C	T	S
O	T	E	O	M	K	J	R	O	E	U	J	L	E	F
P	U	S	G	W	O	T	E	P	G	K	W	G	R	L
K	R	A	S	V	E	A	M	L	O	P	E	R	A	L
A	N	R	I	U	F	R	A	I	S	E	B	A	R	A
V	O	A	N	C	J	H	F	Q	P	U	Z	M	A	L
I	X	M	G	E	B	Z	N	U	E	D	I	M	K	E
L	Y	Q	I	O	Y	S	E	U	L	B	Y	Y	C	A
Z	E	U	N	D	A	O	H	W	U	P	O	S	E	E
E	T	X	G	E	C	I	T	A	L	E	N	T	U	Q

Maria Callas

WHAT DID SHE SAY?

Use the key below to discover the heartfelt words of some extraordinary women.

A	B	C	D	E	F	G
H	I	J	K	L	M	N
O	P	Q	R	S	T	U
	V	W	X	Y	Z	

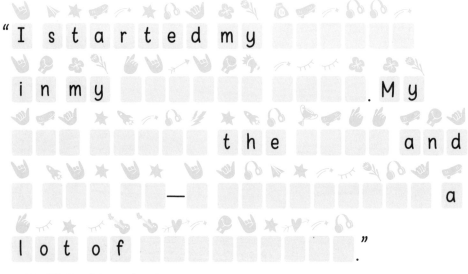

"I started my _____ in my _____. My _____ the _____ and _____ — _____ a lot of _____."

—Steffi Graf, tennis player

"   over a
      is a
                ."

—Reyna Duong, chef

"   ,   in
        , and I   ! It
f e l t   ."

—Mae Jemison, astronaut

"Don't forget to
      with   !
That's where
                "
.

—Niki Yang, animator and voice actor

SKATEBOARDER SWITCHEROO

Skateboarder Sky Brown is always on the move. Looks like her picture doesn't stay put either. Which illustration below is different?

Empress Jingū

REPTILE REDESIGN

Joan Beauchamp Procter was a famous herpetologist. She studied reptiles and amphibians. Study these animals and spot 10 differences in this puzzle.

MEGAN RAPINOE, SOCCER SUPERSTAR

Megan Rapinoe is a champion soccer player. On the field, she runs fast, kicks hard, and is not afraid to change up her game to outsmart her opponents and score goals. She was part of the team that took home the gold medal at the 2012 Olympics and won two World Cup Championships. She uses her fame to speak up for social justice and gender equality. When she scored the winning goal in the 2019 World Cup, the crowd chanted "Equal pay! Equal pay!"

All of the bold words above can be found in the puzzle below. They can go up, down, forward, backward, and even diagonally.

E	S	A	V	O	W	U	R	A	B	T	E	Y	W	Q
I	J	U	S	T	I	C	E	T	Y	E	C	T	A	U
V	T	C	E	O	N	E	D	X	O	A	R	I	J	E
M	I	H	E	S	N	U	J	I	C	M	U	L	F	G
X	Y	A	U	K	I	C	K	S	P	E	F	A	L	B
A	B	M	B	I	N	X	O	K	L	U	Z	U	L	O
R	A	P	O	R	G	A	M	E	A	A	K	Q	A	J
E	F	I	S	A	C	E	W	F	Y	N	O	E	L	A
D	E	O	V	U	T	D	S	H	E	R	G	G	E	L
H	S	N	U	R	I	A	Z	O	R	M	L	O	A	I
T	R	G	W	O	R	L	D	C	U	P	W	L	E	M
Y	O	L	Y	M	P	I	C	S	A	V	I	D	Q	U

METAMORPHA-MAZE!

Maria Sibylla Merian observed caterpillars and butterflies to learn all about metamorphosis. She published books filled with her beautiful, detailed drawings to teach other people what she knew. Trace a path through this maze to help Maria reach the butterfly.

ANSWER KEY

4–5: WHAT MAKES A REBEL A REBEL?

```
A V F I W G X D J I A Q W O L
C O M M U N I T I E S C A L H
H I C G U B L C S R A T S E I
A C S A E N U R K E P J F A N
L E R X D P V E V B Q S L D G
L S K E J A H A Z E S T L E E
E B I R L O R T F L T R A R N
N E N O U B G I K C O E C S U
G J D C Q M O V U W Y N E H I
E I N S P I R I N G R G A I T
S H E R A B K T S W Z T E P Y
F O S B O L D Y X D R H Q A O
U E S V E J B N W E D V H O M
L H I K E C N E I L I S E R G
P O Z A L T S A X C W K U D B
```

6–7: WHAT'S COOKING?

8: SPOT THE IMPOSTER

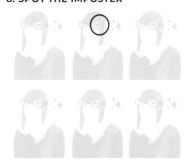

10–11: READY TO RHYME?

WORE
CHORE
SCORE
SHORE
ROAR

MORE
BEFORE
DOOR TO DOOR
WAR

12: CLIMB A WORD LADDER!

READ
BEAD
BEAT

BOAT
BOOT
BOOK

14–15: CRACK THE CODE

"As you GROW OLDER, you WILL DISCOVER that you have TWO HANDS: one for HELPING YOURSELF, the other for HELPING OTHERS."
—Audrey Hepburn, actress

"I'd rather FAIL TRYING to DO SOMETHING GOOD in the WORLD than SUCCEED at DOING NOTHING."
—Nadine Burke Harris, pediatrician

"Be STRONG, be GENTLE, be BEAUTIFUL."
—Keiko Fukuda, judo master

"The ONLY THING that can IMPEDE ME is MYSELF."
—Amanda Gorman, poet

16: MODEL MIX-UP

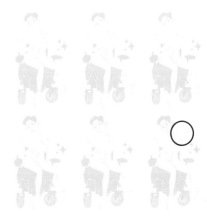

18: MEET CARMEN MIRANDA

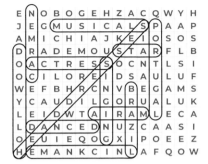

19: SPORTS SCRAMBLE!

LWBINGO = BOWLING
MWSI = SWIM
GISNIK = SKIING
CORK BEMICRL = ROCK CLIMBER
RAWOBODSN = SNOWBOARD
ABBELLSA = BASEBALL
GUEFRI KTASE = FIGURE SKATE
OLFG = GOLF
KATBEBSLAL = BASKETBALL

20: PATH TO THE WHITE HOUSE

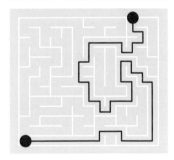

22–23: WISE WORDS

"WINNING the PRIZE wasn't HALF as
EXCITING as DOING the WORK ITSELF."
—Maria Goeppert Mayer, theoretical physicist

"There is SOMETHING DELICIOUS about
WRITING the FIRST WORDS of a STORY. You
NEVER QUITE KNOW WHERE they'll TAKE YOU."
—Beatrix Potter, author and illustrator

"SURROUND YOURSELF with POSITIVE
PEOPLE who are going to LIFT YOU UP."
—Velma Scantlebury, transplant surgeon

24: GRACE HOPPER, COMPUTER PIONEER

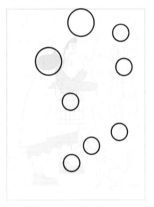

26–27: DIG IT!

28: ADVENTURE JUMBLE

TOUNSMAIN = MOUNTAINS
ESAS = SEAS
UGSELJN = JUNGLES
TNOHR LEOP = NORTH POLE
COSLENOVA = VOLCANOES
CONASE = OCEANS
FWILIDEL = WILDLIFE
SPAM = MAPS
TEEDSSR = DESERTS

30–31: TIME TO RHYME!

SMOKE	CLOAK	BROKE
YOLK	BACKSTROKE	WOKE
OAK	SPOKE	

32: BUILD A WORD LADDER!

SAIL	TALL	TEAL
TAIL	TELL	HEAL

34–35 ASTRONAUT ADJUSTMENTS

36: ARETHA FRANKLIN, QUEEN OF SOUL

```
M A P I N R T A I Z O B K A W
I Y R U P O P F Z H D A G H A
V S P C A C U A M U S I C T S
O T E O M K J R O E U J L E F
P U S G W O T E P G K W G R L
K R A S V E A M L O P E R A L
A N R I U F R A I S E B A R A
V O A N C J H F Q P U Z M A L
I X M G E B Z N U E D I M K E
L Y Q I O Y S E U L B Y Y C A
Z E U N D A O H W U P O S E E
E T X G E C I T A L E N T U Q
```

38–39: WHAT DID SHE SAY?

"I started my CAREER in my LIVING ROOM. My DAD THREW the BALL and I HIT IT—I DESTROYED a lot of FURNITURE."
—Steffi Graf, tennis player

"BONDING over a MEAL TOGETHER is a UNIVERSAL LANGUAGE."
—Reyna Duong, chef

"YES, YOU CAN DANCE in SPACE, and I DID! It felt VERY FREE."
—Mae Jemison, astronaut

"Don't forget to HAVE FUN with WHAT YOU DO! That's where TRUE CREATIVITY comes from."
—Niki Yang, animator and voice actor

40: SKATEBOARDER SWITCHEROO

42–43: REPTILE REDESIGN

44: MEGAN RAPINOE, SOCCER SUPERSTAR

```
E S A V O W U R A B T E Y W Q
I J U S T I C E T Y E C T A U
V T C E O N E D X O A R I J E
M I H E S N U J I C M U L F G
X Y A U K I C K S P E F A L B
A B M B I N X O K L U Z U L O
R A P O R G A M E A A K Q A J
E F I S A C E W F Y N O E L A
D E O V U T D S H E R G G E L
H S N U R I A Z O R M L O A I
T R G W O R L D C U P W L E M
Y O L Y M P I C S A V I D Q U
```

45: METAMORPHA-MAZE!

DREAM BIGGER * AIM HIGHER * STAY REBEL!

ILLUSTRATION CREDITS:

Elisabetta Stoinich (Ada Lovelace), Helena Morais Soares (Frida Kahlo), Monica Garwood (Helen Keller), Emmanuelle Walker (Jane Goodall), Maliha Abidi (Muzoon Almellehan), Sara Bondi (Malala Yousafzai), Debora Guidi (Khoudia Diop), T.S. Abe (Oprah Winfrey), Giorgia Marras (Qiu Jin), Monica Ahanonu (Lupita Amondi Nyong'o), Elena De Santi (Marjane Satrapi), Veronica Carratello (Nadine Burke Harris), Petra Braun (Yuan Yuan Tan), Paola Rollo (Eufrosina Cruz), Nicole Miles (Kamala Harris), Kelsee Thomas (Stacey Abrams), Alexandra Bowman (Wilma Mankiller), Salini Perera (Chloe Kim), Kate Prior (Sky Brown), Cristina Spanò (Madam C.J. Walker), Thandiwe Tshabalala (Wangari Maathai), Kathrin Honesta (Sonia Sotomayor), Sarah Madden (Lady Gaga)

> *Kindness heals the world. Kindness heals people. It's what brings us together— it's what keeps us healthy.*
>
> **LADY GAGA**

I do know one thing about me: I don't measure myself by others' expectations or let others define my worth.

SONIA SOTOMAYOR

*There are opportunities even in the most
difficult moments.*

WANGARI MAATHAI

I got my start by giving myself a start.

MADAM CJ WALKER

It's OK to fall sometimes. I'm just going to get back up and push even harder.

SKY BROWN

The one thing I learned is to just give everything a shot. You don't want to live with regret.

CHLOE KIM

The most fulfilled people are the ones who get up every morning and stand for something larger than themselves.

WILMA MANKILLER

Leadership is about answering that question: How can I help?

STACEY ABRAMS

**While I may be the first woman in this office,
I won't be the last.**

KAMALA HARRIS

When a woman decides to change,
everything changes around her.

EUFROSINA CRUZ

To be perfect is impossible, but to be better is possible. When I look back and see that I'm better than yesterday, then it's good enough.

YUAN YUAN TAN

> *I'd rather fail trying to do something good in the world than succeed at doing nothing.*
>
> **NADINE BURKE HARRIS**

One isn't born courageous,
one becomes it.

MARJANE SATRAPI

*No matter where you're from,
your dreams are valid.*

LUPITA AMONDI NYONG'O

*Don't tell me women are not
the stuff of heroes.*

QIU JIN

> **You get in life what you have the courage to ask for.**
>
> **OPRAH WINFREY**

If you're lucky enough to be different, don't ever change.

KHOUDIA DIOP

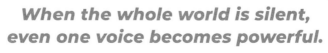

When the whole world is silent,
even one voice becomes powerful.

MALALA YOUSAFZAI

In the middle of the darkness,
learning gives you light.

MUZOON ALMELLEHAN

> *Only if we understand, will we care. Only if we care, will we help. Only if we help, shall all be saved.*

JANE GOODALL

> *The best and most beautiful things in the world cannot be seen or touched, but they must be felt with the heart.*

HELEN KELLER

*Feet, what do I need you for when
I have wings to fly?*

FRIDA KAHLO

> **That brain of mine is something more than merely mortal, as time will show.**
>
> **ADA LOVELACE**

THIS BOOK BELONGS TO

_____

_____